The Credit Crunch Christian

27 Ways to Lookup
When Things are Looking Down

Dr Richard de Lisser

© Copyright
Dr Richard de Lisser 2009

All rights reserved. No part of this publication may be reproduced, stored in an information or retrieval system, or transmitted in any form or by any means, electronic or mechanical including photocopying or recording without the prior permission in writing of the publisher, nor be otherwise circulated in any form of binding or cover other than that in which it is published.

First Produced, 2009

Most, but not all of the Scripture quotations are taken
from the New American Standard Bible.

British Library Cataloguing in Publication Data.
A catalogue record for this book is available from the British Library.

ISBN 978-0-9562783-0-2

Author
Dr Richard de Lisser

Published By
FOR ALL OCCASIONS
High Wycombe

Printed in the UK

Cover Artwork © Shutterstock / James Thew
Design & Layout, Daren Bullock, For All Occasions

In September 2005 the SEC executive committee invited him to serve as Personal Ministries and Sabbath School director for the Conference. In 2007 he was elected to serve as Communication and Stewardship director for the Conference.

Dr. Richard de Lisser is married to Joanne Graham-de Lisser, a health professional, and God has gifted them with a 3 year old son, Akala Joshua Alexander de Lisser.

Dedicated to

Joanne my wife
&
Akala our son

About the Author

Introduction - Page 7
Before We Begin – Page 8

1. *Don't Panic* – Pages 9
2. *Don't Worry* – Pages 12
3. *This is a Season* – Pages 18
4. *Share* – Pages 22
5. *Faithfulness* – Pages 26
6. *Waste Not Want Not* – Pages 29
7. *Build a Budget* – Pages 33
8. *Be Honest in your Business* – Pages 43
9. *Be Content* – Pages 50
10. *Get Out of Debt!* – Pages 57
11. *Getting Rich Quick* – Pages 62
12. *Don't Give Up on Giving Up* - Pages 67
13. *Invest Wisely* – Pages 75
14. *Lending & Helping* – Pages 79
15. *The Love of Money* – Pages 85
16. *Have a Plan* – Pages 89
17. *God Will Provide* – Pages 96
18. *Prosper* – Pages 99
19. *Receive* – Pages 105
20. *Save* – Pages 107
21. *Strive for Success* – Pages 109
22. *Being a Guarantor* – Pages 113
23. *Satisfy Your Need Not Your Greed!* – Pages 115
24. *Returning the Tithe* – Pages 117
25. *Lets Get to Work* – Pages 124
26. *Grow your Own* – Pages 131
27. *Give Thanks* – Page 135

Conclusion – Page 136

About the Author

Dr. Richard J. de Lisser is a fourth generation Seventh-day Adventist (SDA) and was baptised in 1978 by the late Pastor Theodore McLeary. Having worked as an administrative officer to the Secretary of State for Education, Lord Baker of Dorking, he responded to the call to enter Gospel ministry and undertook his ministerial training at West Indies College (now Northern Caribbean University), graduating in 1991 as senior class president with a BA in Religion. In 1993 he graduated from Newbold College with a MA in Religion from Andrews University.

He commenced ministerial service in the South England Conference of Seventh–day Adventists (SEC) as an intern at the Holloway church in July 1993. In 1994 he was asked to serve as the pastor for the New Life and the Tottenham Holcombe Road churches (1994-1999), as well as chaplain of the John Loughborough School

(1994-1998). In 1998 he was asked to serve as the North London district coordinator and conducted and coordinated two successful evangelistic campaigns, baptizing over one hundred people. In that same year he was ordained to the Gospel ministry.

In 1999 he completed his doctoral degree and graduated from North Park Theological Seminary Chicago, Illinois, USA. From 1999-2005 he served as the pastor of the Stoke Newington Community SDA church and the Leytonstone Community SDA Church (1999-2003) where he established strong community initiatives. He also served on the SEC Executive Committee from 1999-2007.

From 2001-2005 he served as the chairman of the London Area Advisory Council (LAAC) and led out in two very successful evangelist campaigns: All London All Power with Leo Schriven and Power in the Park with Mildred Robinson, baptizing over 200 people.

Introduction

Credit crunch, economic downturn, recession, depression, bailouts, quantitative easing, repossessions, redundancy, rate cuts, stimulus packages, liquidation, consolidation, debt, liquidity, inflation, deflation, bankruptcy, instability, stock market decline, and more, are all phrases that we have become familiar with! We are facing the worst economic crisis in the world's history. Economists and politicians alike are at a loss on how to navigating the world out of this mess. As British Prime Minister Gordon Brown said, 'there is no historical reference, no road map for getting out of this current global crisis.'

For the Christian, however, there is a way out! The Bible continues to be the Christian's compass and road map in navigating through this financial storm. If we take heed the current crisis can be an opportunity to prove that God is really in control! How can we handle the current credit crunch crisis and survive and thrive? Here are 27 ways!

Before We Begin

In the most part, I have used the New American Standard Bible for the verses quoted with some other versions as well. You may choose your own version to read if that helps you to understand better. Read as you wish: one section a day or in one or two sittings. Feel comfortable to ponder or to pace your way through…but remember to share what you have found and be a blessing to others.

1. Don't Panic

Panic is defined as a sudden overwhelming feeling of terror or anxiety, sometimes affecting a whole group of people. The first thing not to do in a crisis is to panic! Too many people are panicking over a situation that they have no control over and they are getting themselves deeper and deeper into a state of despair. STOP! Calm down and read God's panacea for panicking souls, Psalm 46 1-3, God is our refuge and strength, a very present help in trouble. Therefore we will not fear, though the earth should change and though the mountains slip into the heart of the sea; though its waters roar and foam, though the mountains quake at its swelling pride.

Today we are witnessing a global pandemic in panicking with stories that are shocking the world. One such story in a Los Angeles suburb, is of a father, apparently upset over the loss of his job, who shot dead his wife and five children before killing himself in a Los Angeles suburb. Another story is that of a family of four in Ohio who were murdered by their father/husband who subsequently killed himself because it is speculated that he had lost his job. These stories may seem a little extreme but when we don't have an anchor in God anything can happen.

People panic over things they have no control over. Take, for instance, a recent story about a lady called Karla. She lives in Texas, where thunderstorms and tornadoes are practically a way of life, yet she is deathly afraid of thunder and especially the threat of tornadoes. So, one Saturday afternoon she was napping upstairs in her room when a great thunderstorm woke her. She ran downstairs to find nobody around. Her entire family had seemingly vanished into thin air. She'd been told her whole life that tornadoes sound like a freight train when they hit the ground and she was sure she could hear something chugging away outside her front door.

She'd also been told her whole life that when a tornado hits, the best thing to do is to take shelter in an interior space with no windows. Panicked, she rushed into the pantry right off the kitchen and crouched on the floor with huge sacks of rice and flour all around her. That is where her two older brothers, mom and dad found her, about 10 minutes later, moaning and crying. Her family had been on the back porch observing a mild thunderstorm in full swing. They all laughed hysterically at her antics and just chalked the whole thing up to panic.

The financial thunderstorm is underway! Stop! Don't panic! God is still in control!

2. Don't Worry

Worry is defined as, to be, or cause to be anxious or uneasy. There are some people in this world who are so worried, that when they are not worried, they are worried by the fact that they are not worried! This is not a time to worry. This is a time of opportunity, to get closer to God and build on our relationship with Him, to offload our cares on Him. See Matt 6:30-32, But if God so clothes the grass of the field, which is alive today and tomorrow is thrown into the furnace, will He not much more clothe you? You of little faith! Do not worry then, saying, 'What will we eat?' or 'What will we drink?' or 'What will we wear for clothing?' For the Gentiles eagerly seek all these things; for your heavenly Father knows that you need all these things.

Hannah Whitehall Smith wrote an inspiring quote in the book, *The Christian's Secret of a Happy Life*: You find no difficulty in trusting the Lord with the management of the universe, and all the outward creation, and can your case be any more complex or difficult than these, that you need to be anxious or troubled about His management of you? Away with such unworthy doubting! Take your stand on the power and trustworthiness of your God, and see how quickly all difficulties will vanish before a steadfast determination to believe. Trust in the dark, trust in the light, trust at night and trust in the morning, and you will find that the faith which may begin by mighty effort will end sooner or later by becoming the easy and natural habit of the soul. (Cited in James Blanchard Cisneros' *You Have Chosen to Remember*, p.147)

Winston Churchill once said, "When I look back on all these worries, I remember the story of the old man who said on his deathbed that he had had a lot of trouble in his life, most of which never happened."

Don't worry; it may never happen and even

if it does, God will be right there to take you through it!

God's Word on the Matter:

Isaiah 51:12
I, even I, am He who comforts you, who are you that you are afraid of man who dies and of the son of man who is made like grass

Matthew 6:25
For this reason I say to you, do not be worried about your life, as to what you will eat or what you will drink; nor for your body, as to what you will put on. Is not life more than food, and the body more than clothing? "Look at the birds of the air, that they do not sow, nor reap nor gather into barns, and yet your heavenly Father feeds them. Are you not worth much more than they? And who of you by being worried can add a single hour to his life?

Matthew 6:31-33
Do not worry then, saying, "What will we eat?" or "What will we drink?"' or "What will we wear for clothing?" For the Gentiles eagerly seek all these things; for your heavenly Father knows that you need all these things. But seek first His kingdom and His righteousness, and all these things will be added to you.

Matthew 6:34
So do not worry about tomorrow; for tomorrow will care for itself. Each day has enough trouble of its own.

Luke 12:22-29
And He said to His disciples, "For this reason I say to you, do not worry about your life, as to what you will eat; nor for your body, as to what you will put on. For life is more than food, and the body more than clothing? Consider the ravens, for they neither sow nor reap; they have no storeroom nor barn, and yet God feeds them; how much more valuable you are than the

birds! And which of you by worrying can add a single hour to his lifespan? If then you cannot do even a very little thing, why do you worry about other matters? Consider the lilies, how they grow: they neither toil nor spin; but I tell you, not even Solomon in all his glory clothed himself like one of these. But if God so clothes the grass in the field, which is alive today and tomorrow is thrown into the furnace, how much more will He clothe you? You men of little faith! And do not seek what you will eat and what you will drink, and do not keep worrying.

Philippians 4:6
Be anxious for nothing, but in everything by prayer and supplication with thanksgiving let your requests be made known to God.

Hebrews 13:6
So that we confidently say, "The Lord is my helper, I will not be afraid. What will man do to me?"

1 Peter 5:7
Casting all your anxiety on Him, because He cares for you.

3. This is a Season

A season is defined as a definite or indefinite period of time. Just like Spring follows Winter and Autumn Summer, the world is passing through a season that will come to pass. It might be a long season, some may have seen green shots of recovery already, but we are assured that as day follows night this season will come to pass as the wise man Solomon said in Ecclesiastes 3:1, There is an appointed time for everything. And there is a time for every event under heaven.

This season has been allotted to us for a purpose. Nothing that we go through happens by chance, but has been permitted for a reason. There is a reason for this season in our lives! What can we learn from this? In order to learn the lesson from this season and to use it to our advantage and benefit we must ask God to show us what we must do. It will come to pass and there are those who will emerge from this season stronger and wiser and those who will have been submerged by the torrent and never recover.

Where will you be when this is all over?

His name was Victor, but he felt like a loser. He didn't do very well in school. When he was 16 years old, a teacher advised him to drop out of high school and get a job. He didn't do much better in the working world so that by the time he was 32, he had failed at 76 different jobs.

But applying for job number 77 was to change Victor's life. As part of the interview process, he was required to take an I.Q. test - a test designed to measure his intelligence. A score of 100 was considered to be normal. Victor scored 161. He had never before realized it, but Victor was a genius. The knowledge of that fact transformed his life. Victor Serienko went on to become famous for his research in laser surgery and to become president of MENSA, an organisation for geniuses - all because a test said that he was special.

God sends different seasons to teach us different lessons. We don't know what is in us unless the seasons expose our character. Seasons help us to learn how we cope in times of trial, times of prosperity, times of doubt and financial turmoil.

How long will this season last? I am not one to predict the length of this recession, but there are some who have predicted that recovery is on its way. What I will say is that this season will come to pass eventually. However, even though things may seem to get back to normal, this season may very well be the precursor to the coming of Jesus Christ…

The world as we know it has changed, things will never be the same again. As Christians we must rely on a God who will never change, as He is the same yesterday, today and forever. Trust

Him. This is a season learn from it!

God's Word on the Matter:

Hebrews 13:8
Jesus Christ is the same yesterday, today and forever. (Living Bible)

4. Share

The word share is defined as a part or portion of something that belongs to or is contributed by a person or group. In a little district called Moneague in the parish of St Ann, Jamaica lived a lady by the name of Merita Charles, my Grandmother. Now ninety-eight years old, she has never stopped sharing what she has. I would walk into her kitchen and wonder, 'How is Gran going to cook for all these hungry people?' To my eyes there was nothing in the kitchen that even looked like it could be cooked yet alone feed the 5,000! But as she walked into the kitchen shooing the grandchildren out of the way, she was to perform a culinary miracle that would have us wanting more of her delicious meal. Grandma Charles knew how to share the little that she had and God blessed it! She may not have much but she knows a God who has everything.

God's Word on the Matter:

How can we share when we have less and still end up with more? Ask the women who Elijah met:

1st Kings 17:8-16
Then the word of the LORD came to him: "Go at once to Zarephath of Sidon and stay there. I have commanded a widow in that place to supply you with food." So he went to Zarephath. When he came to the town gate, a widow was there gathering sticks. He called to her and asked, "Would you bring me a little water in a jar so I may have a drink?" As she was going to get it, he called, "And bring me, please, a piece of bread." "As surely as the LORD your God lives," she replied, "I don't have any bread—only a handful of flour in a jar and a little oil in a jug. I am gathering a few sticks to take home and make a meal for myself and my son, that we may eat it—and die." Elijah said to her, "Don't be afraid. Go home and do as you have

said. But first make a small cake of bread for me from what you have and bring it to me, and then make something for yourself and your son. For this is what the LORD, the God of Israel, says: 'The jar of flour will not be used up and the jug of oil will not run dry until the day the LORD gives rain on the land.' "She went away and did as Elijah had told her. So there was food every day for Elijah and for the woman and her family. 16 For the jar of flour was not used up and the jug of oil did not run dry, in keeping with the word of the LORD spoken by Elijah.

This is a miracle that can only encourage us in these times of austerity, to believe that when we share more will be given to us.

In the book of Acts, the New Testament church facing persecution, recession and depression came alive and thrived on the principle of sharing:

Acts 4:32-35

And the congregation of those who believed were of one heart and soul; and not one of them claimed that anything belonging to him was his own, but all things were common property to them. And with great power the apostles were giving testimony to the resurrection of the Lord Jesus, and abundant grace was upon them all. For there was not a needy person among them, for all who were owners of land or houses would sell them and bring the proceeds of the sales and lay them at the apostles' feet, and they would be distributed to each as any had need.

During this time of recession with homes being repossessed, people losing their jobs, and people being in need, should we not as a church both individually and collectively share what we have with each other so that no one is in need?

This was the power of the New Testament church. It can be ours today if we would but share!

5. Faithfulness

Faithfulness can be defined as, adhering firmly and devotedly to someone or something that elicits or demands one's fidelity. Faith is a hard commodity to find in our faithless age, but as Christians we are called to have faith in the good times as well as in the bad, for the One in whom we place our faith and our trust is ever faithful. Lamentation 3:22-24 says, The LORD'S loving kindnesses indeed never cease, For His compassions never fail. They are new every morning; Great is Your faithfulness. The LORD is my portion, says my soul, therefore I have hope in Him, for His mercies are new every morning!

The song writer says; Great is Thy faithfulness, O God my Father...Morning by morning new mercies I see. All I have needed Thy hand hath provided. Great is Thy faithfulness, Lord, unto me.

During these testing times we are called to have faith, not to fear, because faithfulness has its rewards. As God's stewards we are called to be faithful in the small things as well as in the big things.

A little boy asked his father, "Dad, if three frogs were sitting on a limb that hung over a pond, and one frog decided to jump off the limb and into the pond, how many frogs would be left on the limb?"

The dad replied, "Two frogs."

"No," the son replied. "Let me ask you again. There's three frogs and one decides to jump into the pond, how many are left?"

The dad sais, "Oh, I get it, if one decides to jump, the others would jump too. So there are none left."

The boy said, "No dad, that's not right. The

answer is three frogs. The frog only DECIDED to jump - he never did jump."

This is not a time to jump! Whatever you have decided, hang on in there, help is on it's way!

In these times God does not require you to be brilliant. God does not require you to be clever. God does not require you to be articulate. God does not require you to be innovative. God does not require you to be charming. God does not require you to be handsome or beautiful. But He does require you to be faithful.

6. Waste Not Want Not

Waste can be defined as, to use, consume, spend, or expend thoughtlessly or carelessly. If we don't waste what we have, we will still have it in the future and will not lack it.

In times of plenty there is a tendency to waste. By the same degree, in times of scarcity, there is a tendency to save. As a child growing up my parents would always repeat this time old phrase; 'waste not, want not', particularly at mealtimes when invariable my siblings and I would leave food on our plates. My mother would remind us of the starving children in Africa in a hope that that would jolt the bone of compassion in us to be grateful for what we had. This often did the trick.

The Independent Newspaper reported the following:

From entire crops of barely blemished potatoes, to shelves of supermarket sandwiches on their sell-by dates, it is a roll call of waste created by one nation that could lift 150 million people from starvation in one year. The ability of Britons to throw away food deemed imperfect, out-of-date or surplus to requirements was put into sharp relief with the revelation that 30 to 40% of all produce is simply binned. Research based on government statistics has found that, every year, food worth £20 billion is discarded on its journey from the farmyard to the fridge. £20 billion of discarded food is equivalent to almost five times what Britain spent last year on international aid, including the amount of debt relief to the world's poorest countries. The average British adult throws away £420 of food a year!

The Japanese have a word called, *Mottainai*. It is a term meaning a sense of regret concerning waste when the intrinsic value of an object or resource is not properly utilized. The expression,

"Mottainai!" can be uttered as an exclamation when something useful, such as food or time, is wasted.

As Christians we live with a sense of responsibility and accountability.

God's Word on the Matter:

Luke 15:13-14
He squandered his estate with loose living. Now when he had spent everything, a severe famine occurred in that country and he began to be impoverished. (one situation where the word, *Mottainai* would have been very apt)

Luke 12:48
From everyone who has been given much, much will be required.

John 6:12
When they were filled, He said to His disciples, "Gather up the leftover fragments so that

nothing will be lost."

We have a responsibility not to waste anything whether it be food, energy, water or any other resource or commodity, for we live not unto ourselves but for the security of future generations.

7. Build a Budget

Budgeting is simply defined as a process of planning our expenses to be equal to or less than our income. Some may prefer to use the phrase, a spending plan, but whatever way you wish to describe it a budget allows us to see how much we have and how much we will need to spend in any given period of time (such as a week, month or year).

As Christians, God wants us to plan. God does not want us to be slaves to sin or man. When debt becomes more than we can bear, it leaves us in bondage. Budgets help us to prevent this by showing what we can afford and prevent us from taking on more than we can handle.

Do you find yourself with too little money left at the end of the month? Many Christian families live above their income. A recent survey indicates that 80% of Christian families spend in excess of their incomes. Many are not even aware of the limitations of their their income. Their only limit is on their credit cards.

Someone has said: "We live in plentiful poverty - one paycheque removed from bankruptcy." Financial difficulties are major contributing factors in separation and divorces.

Why Have a Budget?

A budget properly used won't enslave you - it will make you free. It doesn't take money away from you; it gives you more money to use for what you want. It helps you to know where you stand and what progress you're making toward your goals. (Ed Reid, North American Division Stewardship Director)

Other reasons for having a budget include the following:

1. To organise your giving to God
2. To have money for the unexpected
3. To help one get out of debt
4. To help provide for educational expenses
5. To help provide for future retirement
6. To unite the family in decision making
7. To help in role modeling for your children
8. To be accountable as God's Stewards

Money Management Principles and Reflecting God in Family Budgeting:

1. Put God First:

Proverbs 3:9 Honour the LORD from your wealth and from the first of all your produce.

- Surrender ownership to God
- Explore Biblical criteria and principles

- In consultation with the Holy Spirit, establish lifestyle boundaries as a family
- Manage in partnership with God

2. Consider your household and involve the whole family:

1 Timothy 5:8 says, A Christian who does not take care of his family is worse than an infidel.

- Ask 'What does our family need?' focusing on the necessities of shelter, recreation, food, transportation, clothing and education
- Husbands and wives should talk freely and openly about their financial objectives
- Engaged couples should include finance in their discussions
- Children should be involved in family financial matters
- Establish goals and objectives as a family

- Determine where you are
- Be informed on family financial planning
- Maintain an expenditure diary which includes:
    - total expenses including variables
    - total income
    - lists of all debts

3. Consider the world

- Give to support the work of the Gospel Ministry
- Contribute to Global Mission work
- Give for the maintenance and upkeep of the Church
- Assist the poor and those less unfortunate than yourself

4. Spend no more than you receive

- "Owe no man any thing." (Romans 13:8)

5. Avoid Debts

Ellen White states, You must see that one should not manage his affairs in a way that will incur debt...When one becomes involved in debt, he is in one of Satan's nets, which he sets for souls.

Abstracting and using money for any purpose, before it is earned, is a snare...Be determined never to incur another debt. Deny yourself a thousand things rather than run in debt... Make a solemn covenant with God that by His blessing you will pay your debts and then owe no man anything if you live on porridge and bread. *Adventist Home*, pp.392-393

6. Face facts

- Be informed on family financial planning
- Plan a family budget - a good budget is simply good planning
- To have a budget is to direct where you

want your money to go
- Learn how to manage your accounts

All should learn how to keep accounts. Some neglect this work as nonessential, but this is wrong. All expenses should be accurately stated. *Adventist Home*, p.374

Open your account book, and see how your account stands with God, with your household and with the world." OHC, p.192

Joseph Felix, in his book, *It's Easier for a Rich Man to Enter Heaven, Than for a Poor Man to Remain on Earth* states:

"Done correctly, budgeting is an act of humble worship. Making an inventory of our financial resources is an expression of gratitude to the Lord for the good things He has given us to use. We recognize that whatever earning power we have comes from Him and is dependent upon

Him for sustenance. As we look at our needs and identify the things our money will be used for, we apply the values that are consistent with our faith and philosophy."

God's Word on the Matter:

Proverbs 6:6-8
Go to the ant, sluggard; consider her ways and be wise; who having no guide, overseer, or ruler, provides her food in the summer and gathers her food in the harvest.

Proverbs 21:5
The thoughts of the diligent tend only to plenty; but the thoughts of everyone who is hasty only to poverty.

Proverbs 22:3
A prudent one foresees the evil and hides himself, but the simple pass on and are punished.

Proverbs 24:3-4
Through wisdom a house is built, and by understanding it is established; and by knowledge the rooms shall be filled with all precious and pleasant riches.

Proverbs 25:28
He who has no rule over his own spirit is like a broken down city without a wall.

Proverbs 27:12
A prudent man sees evil and hides himself, the naive proceed and pay the penalty.

Proverbs 27:23
Know well the face of your flocks; and pay attention to your herds.

Proverbs 27:26
The lambs are for your clothing, and the goats are the price of the field.

Luke 14:28-30
For which of you, intending to build a tower, does not sit down first and count the cost, whether he may have enough to finish it; lest perhaps, after he has laid the foundation and is not able to finish, all those seeing begin to mock him, saying, This man began to build and was not able to finish.

1 Corinthians 16:2
On the first day of every week each one of you is to put aside and save, as he may prosper, so that no collections be made when I come.

8. Be Honest in your Business

Today much blame has been cast at the feet of the bankers for the current credit crunch crisis, where their honesty and integrity have been called into question. As Christians we are called to a higher level of accountability and transparency in all levels of secular and spiritual business. Business drives our economy but honesty drives our inner life. As we undertake our daily activities and enter into our routine transactions in this current climate, it is necessary that our integrity remains intact and God will bless our endeavours.

At the time of writing the scandal with MP's expenses is very much in the news with Fleet Street turning the spotlight on those who govern us. It is no wonder why the British public have became more and more apathetic, as politics becomes a dirty word once again, as MP's feather their own nests during a time of need.

2 Corinthians 8:21 reminds us, For we have regard for what is honorable, not only in the sight of the Lord, but also in the sight of men.

Honesty is still the best policy for this is the way of Christ, He was poor, He had nowhere to lay His head but yet He was careful to owe no man anything. He paid His taxes and even paid for someone else, such was His honesty and integrity.

Our religion will be judged by the world based upon our ethics and our moral standing. The world watches our character keenly, closely and carefully to find out if we are honourable and true to our word, and if we are it will speak well of our religion and Jesus, who we serve. However, if we have been dishonest we will have little rest or peace, for our conscience will condemn us, our thoughts will trouble and distress us and our faith will shrink amidst fear and forboding. But God is able to forgive once we have confessed and put us back on the path of honesty where we can live at peace with ourselves once more. It pays to be honest.

An unknown author wrote, It is better to lose with a conscience clean than to win with a trick unfair; It is better to fail, and to know you've been, whatever the prize was, square. Than to claim the joy of a far-off goal and the cheer of the standers-by, and to know down deep in your inmost soul, a cheat you must live and die.

God's Word on the Matter:

Leviticus 19:13
You shall not oppress your neighbor, nor rob him. The wages of a hired man are not to remain with you all night until morning.

Deuteronomy 25:13-15
You shall not have in your bag differing weights, a large and a small. You shall not have in your house differing measures, a large and a small. You shall have a full and just weight; you shall

have a full and just measure, that your days may be prolonged in the land which the LORD your God gives you.

Job 31:13-14
"If I have despised the claim of my male or female slaves when they filed a complaint against me, what then could I do when God arises? And when He calls me to account, what will I answer Him?"

Psalm 112:5
It is well with the man who deals generously and lends, who conducts his affairs with justice.

Proverbs 10:4
Poor is he who works with a negligent hand, but the hand of the diligent makes rich.

Proverbs 11:1
A false balance is an abomination to the LORD, but a just weight is His delight.

Proverbs 13:4
The soul of the sluggard craves and gets nothing, but the soul of the diligent is made fat.

Proverbs 13:11
Wealth obtained by fraud dwindles, but the one who gathers by labor increases it.

Proverbs 16:8
Better is a little with righteousness than great income with injustice.

Proverbs 22:16
He who oppresses the poor to make more for himself or who gives to the rich, will only come to poverty.

Jeremiah 22:13
Woe to him who builds his house without righteousness and his upper rooms without justice, who uses his neighbor's services without pay and does not give him his wages.

Malachi 3:5
Then I will draw near to you for judgment; and I will be a swift witness against the sorcerers and against the adulterers and against those who swear falsely, and against those who oppress the wage earner in his wages, the widow and the orphan, and those who turn aside the alien and do not fear Me, says the LORD of hosts.

Luke 16:10
He who is faithful in a very little thing is faithful also in much; and he who is unrighteous in a very little thing is unrighteous also in much.

Ephesians 6:9
And masters, do the same things to them, and give up threatening, knowing that both their Master and yours is in heaven, and there is no partiality with Him.

Colossians 4:1
Masters, grant to your slaves justice and fairness, knowing that you too have a Master in heaven.

1 Timothy 5:18
For the Scripture says, "Do not muzzle the ox while it is treading out the grain," and "The worker deserves his wages."

James 5:4
Look! The wages you failed to pay the workmen who mowed your fields are crying out against you. The cries of the harvesters have reached the ears of the Lord Almighty.

9. Be Content

We live in an era of discontent, particularly at this time of economic downturn and recession. What with thousands losing their jobs, their homes and their way of life, you can soon see how discontentment can set in. As Christians we are assured from the Word of God that even if we lose all God will take care of us. The Psalmist says in Psalm 121: 1-8, I will lift up my eyes to the mountains; from where shall my help come? My help comes from the LORD, Who made heaven and earth. He will not allow your foot to slip; He who keeps you will not slumber. Behold, He Who keeps Israel will neither slumber nor sleep. The LORD is your keeper; The LORD is your shade on your right hand. The sun will not smite you by day, nor the moon by night. The LORD will protect you from all evil; He will keep your soul. The LORD will guard your going out and your coming in From this time forth and forever.

Coming down the stairs one morning, a British gentleman by the name of Lord Congelton overheard his cook conversing with one of the other servants. "I would be perfectly content," the woman declared, "if I just had five pounds!"

Curious at what a perfectly content person is like, Lord Congelton decided to help his long-time employee. He pulled her aside later in the day and gave her a five-pound note - a fairly substantial sum at the time. The surprised cook thanked her employer profusely, whereupon Lord Congelton departed.

But once outside the door, Congelton paused to see what, if anything, the woman would say. Surely, he reasoned, she would express her thankfulness to God.

A second or two passed and Congelton heard the woman cry out, "Oh, why on earth didn't I say ten pounds?!" *Today in the Word*, 25/06/1996

Quotes on contentment:

"Contentment is a decision to be happy with what you already have."

"Contentment is not receiving the things we want. It is the realization of how much we already have."

"Contentment is when you are happy where you are, with whom you are and who you are."

"True contentment is realizing that life is a gift, not a right."

"If you are content, you have enough to live comfortably." (Plautus)

"Since we cannot get what we like, let us like what we can get." (Spanish Proverb)

"Contentment is natural wealth, luxury is artificial poverty." (Socrates)

"The secret of contentment is knowing how to enjoy what you have, and to be able to lose all desire for things beyond your reach." (Lin Yutang)

"Contentment means that whatever we do not have we do not require." (Alexander McLaren)

"To be content makes a person rich, but to be malcontent makes a rich man poor." (Benjamin Franklin)

"Contentment means satisfaction on the inside, no matter what is going on outside."

God's Word on the Matter:

Psalm 23:1
The Lord is my shepherd, I shall not want.

Ecclesiastes 5:10
Whoever loves money never has money enough; whoever loves wealth is never satisfied with his income. This too is meaningless.

Matthew 6:31-33
"Do not worry then, saying, 'What will we eat?' or 'What will we drink?' or 'What will we wear for clothing?' "For the Gentiles eagerly seek all these things; for your heavenly Father knows that you need all these things. "But seek first His kingdom and His righteousness, and all

these things will be added to you.

Luke 3:14
Some soldiers were questioning him, saying, "And what about us, what shall we do?" And he said to them, "Do not take money from anyone by force, or accuse anyone falsely, and be content with your wages."

Philippians 4:11-13
For I have learned to be content, whatever the circumstances may be. I know now how to live when things are difficult and I know how to live when things are prosperous. In general and in particular I have learned the secret of eating well or going hungry of facing either plenty of poverty. I am ready for anything through the strength of the One who lives within me.

1 Thessalonians 4:11
And to make it your ambition to lead a quiet life and attend to your own business and work with your hands, just as we commanded you…

1 Timothy 6:6
But godliness actually is a means of great gain when accompanied by contentment.

1 Timothy 6:7-10
For we brought nothing into the world, and we can take nothing out of it. But if we have food and clothing, we will be content with that. People who want to get rich fall into temptation and a trap and into many foolish and harmful desires that plunge men into ruin and destruction. For the love of money is a root of all kinds of evil. Some people, eager for money, have wandered from the faith and pierced themselves with many griefs.

Hebrews 13:5
Keep your life free from the love of money, and be content with what you have.

James 4:1-3
What is the source of quarrels and conflicts among you? Is not the source your pleasures

that wage war in your members? You lust and do not have; so you commit murder. You are envious and cannot obtain; so you fight and quarrel. You do not have because you do not ask. You ask and do not receive, because you ask with wrong motives, so that you may spend it on your pleasures.

10. Get Out of Debt!

Debt can be defined as, money, goods, or services owed to other people with payments past their due. Debt is the new slavery of the twenty-first century. Today there are many people who are living way beyond their means and have so enmeshed themselves in debt that they will never in their own lifetime pay off what they owe! Many have bought into a celebrity generated lifestyle that suggests that you can have it all and have it all now. The days of deferred gratification and saving up for what you need are long since behind us. People spend what they don't have on things they don't really need, and get themselves into debt they can ill afford.

It is no wonder that this recession has caused so many people to suffer from depression. If you are enslaved and entrenched in debt it is time to break free. We need to pay off as much of the debt as we can; live within our means and satisfy our need, not our greed.

The Scriptural definition of a debt is the inability to meet obligations agreed upon. In other words, when a person buys something on credit terms, that is not necessarily a debt, it is a contract. But, when the terms of that contract are violated, Scriptural debt occurs. Larry Burkett, *Your Finance in Changing Times*, p.64

The Archbishop of York wrote, "Lifestyle choices, from major decisions such as cars, holidays and homes to the products we buy in the supermarket, all reveal something about our values and principles. Our motivations in saving, and how we approach issues of credit and debt are faith issues just as much as our giving."

Ellen White called debt, One of Satan's nets, which he sets for souls...Be determined never to incur another debt. Deny yourself a thousand things rather than run into debt. *Adventist Home*, p.392

Many, very many, have not so educated themselves that they can keep their expenditures within the limit of their income... They borrow again and again and become overwhelmed in debt, and consequently they become discouraged and disheartened. *Adventist Home*, p.374

...The fact that you are in debt weakens your faith and tends to discourage you, and even the thought of it makes you nearly wild. You need to cut down your expenses and strive to supply this deficiency in your character. You can and should make a determined effort to bring under control your disposition to spend means beyond your income. *Adventist Home*, p.393

One person aptly stated: "I would be delighted to pay as I go, if I could just catch up paying where I went!"

It is time for us to cut up the credit cards, pay by cash and live below our means!

God's Word on the Matter:

Exodus 22:14
If a man borrows anything from his neighbor, and it is injured or dies while its owner is not with it, he shall make full restitution.

Deuteronomy 15:6
For the Lord your God will bless you as He has promised you, and you will lend to many nations, but you will not borrow; and you will rule over many nations, but they will not rule over you.

Deuteronomy 28:12
The Lord will open for you His good storehouse, the heavens, to give rain to your land in its season and to bless all the work of your hand; and you shall lend to many nations, but you shall not borrow.

2 Kings 4:7
Then she came and told the man of God. And he said, "Go, sell the oil and pay your debt, and

you and your sons can live on the rest."

Psalm 37:21
The wicked borrows and does not pay back, but the righteous is gracious and gives.

Proverbs 22:7
The rich rules over the poor, and the borrower becomes the lender's slave.

Proverbs 22:26-27
Do not be a man who strikes hands in pledge or puts up security for debts; if you lack the means to pay, your very bed will be snatched from under you.

Ecclesiastes 5:5
It is better that you should not vow than that you should vow and not pay.

Romans 13:8
Owe nothing to anyone except to love one another; for he who loves his neighbor has fulfilled the law

11. Getting rich quick

Who wants to be a millionaire? I do, I hear you say, but in the real world this invariable does not happen over night. Millions of people play the lottery in the hope that they will one day win and be made an instant millionaire, but only very few realize this dream. Still others, in the hope of getting rich quick, sign up to various schemes promising bountiful returns on modest expenditure. And again their dreams end in tears. For the Christian spiritual riches are far more important than material riches and they actually last forever!

Here are some tips in avoiding get rich quick schemes:s

1. Know Your Limitations
A great part of wisdom is knowing your limitations. If you are not an expert in finances seek the help of someone who is. Many people

have lost money in areas that they know nothing about. Conversely many people have made money in areas that they have a lot of knowledge about. No one would be tricked into investing in a scheme in an area that they have knowledge about.

2. Only Risk What You Can Afford to Lose
It is one thing to speculate with money you can afford to lose but it is quite another thing to speculate with money that does not belong to you. The danger is that not only will you lose your own money but you will have to pay back the money you have borrowed if things go wrong!

3. Invest in Things You Can See
Invest in things that you can see. Most get rich quick schemes deal in intangibles services.

4. Think Slowly, Act Wisely
Many of theses get rich quick schemes play on people's emotions i.e. it's too good an opportunity

to miss or if you don't sign up today someone else will, or this is the last time that we are going to offer this deal! Think slowly, pray about it and act wisely. Adapted from *Crown Financial Ministries* online at www.crown.org

God's Word on the Matter:

Exodus 23:12
Six days do your work, but on the seventh day do not work, so that your ox and your donkey may rest and the slave born in your household, and the alien as well, may be refreshed.

Proverbs 12:11
He who tills his land will have plenty of bread, but he who pursues worthless things lacks sense.

Proverbs 13:11
Wealth obtained by fraud dwindles, but the one who gathers by labor increases it.

Proverbs 13:11
Dishonest money dwindles away, but he who gathers money little by little makes it grow.

Proverbs 14:15
The naive believes everything, but the sensible man considers his steps.

Proverbs 19:2
Also it is not good for a person to be without knowledge, and he who hurries his footsteps errs.

Proverbs 21:5
The plans of the diligent lead surely to advantage, but everyone who is hasty comes surely to poverty.

Proverbs 23:4
Do not weary yourself to gain wealth, cease from your consideration of it.

Proverbs 28:19-20
He who tills his land will have plenty of food, but he who follows empty pursuits will have poverty in plenty. A faithful man will abound with blessings, but he who makes haste to be rich will not go unpunished.

12. Don't Give Up on Giving Up

In times of real hardship you would have guessed that the first thing any right thinking person would do is to look at his or her expenditure and begin to cut back. Many of us have gone through that exercise already, however you would have thought that as a result giving to the church would have declined rapidly. No! In fact, it has been proven that in times of hardship and poverty giving to the church actually goes up! For the Christian knows that as Luke reminds us in Luke 6:38, Give, and it will be given to you. They will pour into your lap a good measure, pressed down, shaken together, and running over. For by your standard of measure it will be measured to you in return. In these times don't give up on giving up!

Ellen White says, Voluntary offerings and the tithe constitute the revenue of the gospel." *Testimonies Volume 5*, p.149 She goes on to state, God tests us here, by committing to us temporal possessions, that our use of these may show whether we can be trusted with eternal riches. *Counsels on Stewardship*, p.22

As all learn the lesson of faithful rendering to God what is His due, He through His providence will enable some to bring princely offerings. He will enable others to make smaller offerings, and the small and the large are acceptable to Him if given with an eye single to His glory. *That I May Know Him*, p.220

God's Word on the Matter:

Deuteronomy 15:10
Give generously to him and do so without a grudging heart; then because of this the Lord your God will bless you in all your work and in everything you put your hand to.

Deuteronomy 16:17
Every man shall give as he is able, according to

the blessing of the LORD your God which He has given you.

1 Chronicles 29:9
Then the people rejoiced because they had offered so willingly, for they made their offering to the Lord with a whole heart, and King David also rejoiced greatly.

Proverbs 3:9-10
Honor the Lord from your wealth and from the first of all your produce; So your barns will be filled with plenty and your vats will overflow with new wine.

Proverbs 3:27
Do not withhold good from those to whom it is due, when it is in your power to do it.

Proverbs 11:24-25
There is one who scatters, and yet increases all the more, and there is one who withholds what is justly due, and yet it results only in want. The

generous man will be prosperous, and he who waters will himself be watered.

Proverbs 21:26
…the righteous gives and does not hold back.

Proverbs 22:9
He who is generous will be blessed, for he gives some of his food to the poor.

Proverbs 28:27
He who gives to the poor will never want, but he who shuts his eyes will have many curses.

Malachi 3:10
"Bring the whole tithe into the storehouse, so that there may be food in My house, and test Me now in this," says the Lord of hosts, "if I will not open for you the windows of heaven and pour out for you a blessing until it overflows.

Matthew 6:3-4
But when you give to the poor, do not let your

left hand know what your right hand is doing, so that your giving will be in secret; and your Father who sees what is done in secret will reward you.

Mark 12:41-44
And He sat down opposite the treasury, and began observing how the people were putting money into the treasury; and many rich people were putting in large sums. A poor widow came and put in two small copper coins, which amount to a cent. Calling His disciples to Him, He said to them, "Truly I say to you, this poor widow put in more than all the contributors to the treasury; for they all put in out of their surplus, but she, out of her poverty, put in all she owned, all she had to live on."

Luke 3:11
And he would answer and say to them, "The man who has two tunics is to share with him who has none; and he who has food is to do likewise."

Luke 6:30
Give to everyone who asks of you, and whoever takes away what is yours, do not demand it back.

Acts 20:35
In everything I showed you that by working hard in this manner you must help the weak and remember the words of the Lord Jesus, that He Himself said, 'It is more blessed to give than to receive.

Romans 12:8
…Or he who exhorts, in his exhortation; he who gives, with liberality; he who leads, with diligence; he who shows mercy, with cheerfulness.

2 Corinthians 9:6-8
Now this I say, he who sows sparingly will also reap sparingly, and he who sows bountifully will also reap bountifully. Each one must do just as he has purposed in his heart, not grudgingly or under compulsion, for God loves a cheerful

giver. And God is able to make all grace abound to you, so that always having all sufficiency in everything, you may have an abundance for every good deed.

2 Corinthians 9:10
Now He who supplies seed to the sower and bread for food will supply and multiply your seed for sowing and increase the harvest of your righteousness;

Galatians 6:7
Do not be deceived, God is not mocked; for whatever a man sows, this he will also reap.

Philippians 4:15-17
And you yourselves also know, Philippians, that at the first preaching of the gospel, after I departed from Macedonia, no church shared with me in the matter of giving and receiving but you alone; for even in Thessalonica you send a gift more than once for my needs. Not that I seek the gift itself, but I seek for the profit which increases to your account.

James 2:15-16

If a brother or sister is without clothing and in need of daily food, and one of you says to them, "Go in peace, be warmed and be filled," and yet you do not give them what is necessary for their body, what use is that?

13. Invest Wisely

Take counsel if you are to invest in these uncertain times and be mindful that there are risks with every investment. Investing can be an effective tool for multiplying a Christian's assets. God does direct many Christians to invest and return the proceeds to His work. In doing so we are actually investing in eternity!

God's Word on the Matter:

Proverbs 15:22
Without consultation, plans are frustrated, but with many counselors they succeed.

Proverbs 24:27
Prepare your work outside and make it ready for yourself in the field; afterwards, then, build your house.

Proverbs 28:20
A faithful man will abound with blessings, but he who makes haste to be rich will not go unpunished.

Proverbs 13:11
Wealth obtained by fraud dwindles, but the one who gathers by labor increases it.

Proverbs 19:2
Also it is not good for a person to be without knowledge, and he who hurries his footsteps errs.

Ecclesiastes 11:2
Divide your portion to seven, or even to eight, for you do not know what misfortune may occur on the earth.

Matthew 25:14-30
For it is just like a man about to go on a journey, who called his own slaves and entrusted his possessions to them. To one he gave five talents,

to another, two, and to another, one, each according to his own ability; and he went on his journey. Immediately the one who had received the five talents went and traded with them, and gained five more talents. In the same manner the one who had received the two talents gained two more. But he who received the one talent went away, and dug a hole in the ground and hid his master's money. Now after a long time the master of those slaves came and settled accounts with them. The one who had received the five talents came up and brought five more talents, saying, 'Master, you entrusted five talents to me. See, I have gained five more talents.' His master said to him, 'Well done, good and faithful slave You were faithful with a few things, I will put you in charge of many things; enter into the joy of your master.' Also the one who had received the two talents came up and said, 'Master, you entrusted two talents to me. See, I have gained two more talents.' His master said to him, 'Well done, good and faithful slave. You were faithful with a few things, I will put you in charge of many things; enter into the joy of your master.' And the one also who had received the one talent came up and said, 'Master, I knew you to be a hard man, reaping where you did not sow and gathering where you scattered no seed. And I was afraid, and went away and hid your talent in the ground. See, you have what is yours.' But his master answered and said to him, 'You wicked, lazy slave, you knew that I reap where I did not sow and gather where I scattered no seed. 'Then you ought to have put my money in the bank, and on my arrival I would have received my money back with interest. Therefore take away the talent from him, and give it to the one who has the ten talents.' For to everyone who has, more shall be given, and he will have an abundance; but from the one who does not have, even what he does have shall be taken away. Throw out the worthless slave into the outer darkness; in that place there will be weeping and gnashing of teeth.

14. Lending & Helping

In these times of great distress, suffering and hardship we as a people must be able to help our fellow men in whatever way we can. Only as we place ourselves in another person's shoes will we soon see, feel and know what is needed to alleviate their suffering. Focusing on the needs of other will ultimately provide for our needs being met. These testing times call for tremendous faith!

God's Word on the Matter:

Exodus 22:25
If you lend money to My people, to the poor among you, you are not to act as a creditor to him; you shall not charge him interest.

Leviticus 25:35-37
Now in case a countryman of yours becomes poor and his means with regard to you falter,

then you are to sustain him, like a stranger or a sojourner, that he may live with you. Do not take usurious interest from him, but revere your God, that your countryman may live with you. You shall not give him your silver at interest, nor your food for gain.

Deuteronomy 15:8
But you shall freely open your hand to him, and shall generously lend him sufficient for his need in whatever he lacks.

Deuteronomy 23:19-20
You shall not charge interest to your countrymen: interest on money, food, or anything that may be loaned at interest. You may charge interest to a foreigner, but to your countrymen you shall not charge interest, so that the Lord your God may bless you in all that you undertake in the land which you are about to enter to possess.

Deuteronomy 24:10
When you make your neighbor a loan of any

sort, you shall not enter his house to take his pledge.

Proverbs 3:27-28
Do not withhold good from those to whom it is due, when it is in your power to do it. Do not say to your neighbor, "Go, and come back, and tomorrow I will give it," when you have it with you.

Psalm 15:5
He does not put out his money at interest, nor does he take a bribe against the innocent. He who does these things will never be shaken.

Psalm 37:26
All day long he is gracious and lends, and his descendants are a blessing.

Psalm 112:5
It is well with the man who is gracious and lends; he will maintain his cause in judgment.

Proverbs 28:8
He who increases his wealth by interest and usury gathers it for him who is gracious to the poor.

Nehemiah 5: 1-13
Now there was a great outcry of the people and of their wives against their Jewish brothers. For there were those who said, "We, our sons and our daughters are many; therefore let us get grain that we may eat and live." There were others who said, "We are mortgaging our fields, our vineyards and our houses that we might get grain because of the famine." Also there were those who said, "We have borrowed money for the king's tax on our fields and our vineyards. Now our flesh is like the flesh of our brothers, our children like their children. Yet behold, we are forcing our sons and our daughters to be slaves, and some of our daughters are forced into bondage already, and we are helpless because our fields and vineyards belong to others." Then I was very angry when I had heard their outcry

and these words. I consulted with myself and contended with the nobles and the rulers and said to them, You are exacting usury, each from his brother!" Therefore, I held a great assembly against them. I said to them, "We according to our ability have redeemed our Jewish brothers who were sold to the nations; now would you even sell your brothers that they may be sold to us?" Then they were silent and could not find a word to say. Again I said, "The thing which you are doing is not good; should you not walk in the fear of our God because of the reproach of the nations, our enemies? And likewise I, my brothers and my servants are lending them money and grain. Please, let us leave off this usury. Please, give back to them this very day their fields, their vineyards, their olive groves and their houses, also the hundredth part of the money and of the grain, the new wine and the oil that you are exacting from them." Then they said, "We will give it back and will require nothing from them; we will do exactly as you say." So I called the priests and took an oath from them that they would do according to this promise. I also shook out the front of my garment and said, "Thus may God shake out every man from his house and from his possessions who does not fulfill this promise; even thus may he be shaken out and emptied." And all the assembly said, "Amen!" And they praised the LORD. Then the people did according to this promise.

Matthew 5:42
Give to him who asks of you, and do not turn away from him who wants to borrow from you.

Luke 6:35
But love your enemies, and do good, and lend, expecting nothing in return; and your reward will be great, and you will be sons of the Most High; for He Himself is kind to ungrateful and evil men.

15. The Love of Money

Money is good! But to some, money is god! In the right hands it can be of benefit, however in the wrong hands it can be a burden. We are to use money for the good and never allow it to become our god, for there lies the root of all evil! 16 of Jesus' parables refer to money or wealth. In the Bible there are 2,325 verses on money, wealth or possessions, but only about 500 on either faith or prayer!

God's Word on the Matter:

Matthew 19:21-26
Jesus said to him, "If you wish to be complete, go and sell your possessions and give to the poor, and you will have treasure in heaven; and come, follow Me." But when the young man heard this statement, he went away grieving; for he was one who owned much property. And Jesus said to His disciples, "Truly I say to you, it is hard for a rich

man to enter the kingdom of heaven. "Again I say to you, it is easier for a camel to go through the eye of a needle, than for a rich man to enter the kingdom of God." When the disciples heard this, they were very astonished and said, "Then who can be saved?" And looking at them Jesus said to them, "With people this is impossible, but with God all things are possible."

Mark 4:19
But the worries of the world, and the deceitfulness of riches, and the desires for other things enter in and choke the word, and it becomes unfruitful.

Mark 8:36
For what does it profit a man to gain the whole world, and forfeit his soul?

1 Timothy 6:9-11
But those who want to get rich fall into temptation and a snare and many foolish and harmful desires which plunge men into ruin

and destruction. For the love of money is a root of all sorts of evil, and some by longing for it have wandered away from the faith and pierced themselves with many griefs. But flee from these things, you man of God, and pursue righteousness, godliness, faith, love, perseverance and gentleness.

James 5:1-6
Come now, you rich, weep and howl for your miseries which are coming upon you. Your riches have rotted and your garments have become moth-eaten. Your gold and your silver have rusted; and their rust will be a witness against you and will consume your flesh like fire. It is in the last days that you have stored up your treasure! Behold, the pay of the laborers who mowed your fields, and which has been withheld by you, cries out against you; and the outcry of those who did the harvesting has reached the ears of the Lord of Sabaoth. You have lived luxuriously on the earth and led a life of wanton pleasure; you have fattened your hearts in a

day of slaughter. You have condemned and put to death the righteous man; he does not resist you.

16. Have a Plan

He or she who fails to plan plans to fail! We will not be able to navigate our way out of this turmoil unless we have a plan. Nothing happens by chance. In times of prosperity we must plan for times of austerity. In times of austerity we must plan for times of prosperity. We must have a plan if we are to achieve.

God's Word on the Matter:

Genesis 41:34-36
Let Pharaoh take action to appoint overseers in charge of the land, and let him exact a fifth of the produce of the land of Egypt in the seven years of abundance. "Then let them gather all the food of these good years that are coming, and store up the grain for food in the cities under Pharaoh's authority, and let them guard it. "Let the food become as a reserve for the land for the seven years of famine which will occur in the

land of Egypt, so that the land will not perish during the famine.

Proverbs 6:6-8
Go to the ant, o sluggard, observe her ways and be wise, which, having no chief, officer or ruler, prepares her food in the summer and gathers her provision in the harvest.

Proverbs 13:16
A wise man thinks ahead; a fool doesn't, and even brags about it!

Proverbs 13:19
Desire realized is sweet to the soul, but it is an abomination to fools to turn away from evil.

Proverbs 15:22
Without consultation, plans are frustrated, but with many counselors they succeed.

Proverbs 16:1
The plans of the heart belong to man, but the

answer of the tongue is from the Lord.

Proverb 16:9
A man's heart deviseth his way: but, the Lord directeth his steps.

Proverbs 20:18
Prepare plans by consultation, and make war by wise guidance.

Proverbs 21:5
The plans of the diligent lead surely to advantage, but everyone who is hasty comes surely to poverty.

Proverbs 22:3
The prudent sees the evil and hides himself, but the naive go on, and are punished for it.

Proverbs 24:3-4
By wisdom a house is built, and by understanding it is established; and by knowledge the rooms are filled with all precious and pleasant riches.

Proverbs 24:27
Prepare your work outside and make it ready for yourself in the field; afterwards, then, build your house.

Proverbs 27:12
A prudent man sees evil and hides himself, the naive proceed and pay the penalty.

Proverbs 27:23
Know well the condition of your flocks, and pay attention to your herds;

Ecclesiastes 11:2
Divide your portion to seven, or even to eight, for you do not know what misfortune may occur on the earth.

Matthew 25:1-13
"Then the kingdom of heaven will be comparable to ten virgins, who took their lamps and went out to meet the bridegroom. Five of them were foolish, and five were prudent. For when the

foolish took their lamps, they took no oil with them, but the prudent took oil in flasks along with their lamps. Now while the bridegroom was delaying, they all got drowsy and began to sleep. But at midnight there was a shout, 'Behold, the bridegroom! Come out to meet him.' Then all those virgins rose and trimmed their lamps. The foolish said to the prudent, 'Give us some of your oil, for our lamps are going out.' But the prudent answered, 'No, there will not be enough for us and you too; go instead to the dealers and buy some for yourselves.' And while they were going away to make the purchase, the bridegroom came, and those who were ready went in with him to the wedding feast; and the door was shut. Later the other virgins also came, saying, 'Lord, lord, open up for us.' But he answered, 'Truly I say to you, I do not know you.' Be on the alert then, for you do not know the day nor the hour."

Luke 12:16-21
And He told them a parable, saying, "The land

of a rich man was very productive. And he began reasoning to himself, saying, 'What shall I do, since I have no place to store my crops?' Then he said, 'This is what I will do: I will tear down my barns and build larger ones, and there I will store all my grain and my goods. And I will say to my soul, "Soul, you have many goods laid up for many years to come; take your ease, eat, drink and be merry."' But God said to him, 'You fool! This very night your soul is required of you; and now who will own what you have prepared?' So is the man who stores up treasure for himself, and is not rich toward God."

Luke 14:28-30
For which one of you, when he wants to build a tower, does not first sit down and calculate the cost to see if he has enough to complete it? "Otherwise, when he has laid a foundation and is not able to finish, all who observe it begin to ridicule him, saying, 'This man began to build and was not able to finish.'"

1 Corinthians 16:1-2
Now concerning the collection for the saints, as I directed the churches of Galatia, so do you also. On the first day of every week each one of you is to put aside and save, as he may prosper, so that no collections be made when I come.

1 Timothy 6:7
For we have brought nothing into the world, so we cannot take anything out of it either.

17. God Will Provide

It is a surety as night follows day that God will provide! If you have lost your job, your home and/or your livelihood be assured that God will provide for He is Jehovah Jireh, our provider!

God has a watch care over our body as well as our souls. He provides bread when we are hungry and our present wants He will surely satisfy. He provides help when we are helpless. Though it may be dark and foreboding, the road may be rough and the steps steep and slippery, God can and will solve all of our difficulties and put our fears to flight. Ultimately He provides our salvation; from the lamb on mount Moriah to the lamb on the cross. After all is said and done it is this provision made for us that will be the best provision yet!

God's Word on the Matter:

Nehemiah 6:9
They were all trying to frighten us, thinking, "Their hands will get too weak for the work, and it will not be completed." But I prayed, "Now strengthen my hands."

Psalm 37:25
I have been young and now I am old, yet I have not seen the righteous forsaken or his descendants begging bread.

Matthew 6:31-32
Do not worry then, saying, 'What will we eat?' or 'What will we drink?' or 'What will we wear for clothing?' For the Gentiles eagerly seek all these things; for your heavenly Father knows that you need all these things.

Matthew 7:11
If you then, being evil, know how to give good gifts to your children, how much more will your

Father who is in heaven give what is good to those who ask Him!

Luke 12:7
Indeed, the very hairs of your head are all numbered. Do not fear; you are more valuable than many sparrows.

John 21:6
And He said to them, "Cast the net on the right-hand side of the boat and you will find a catch." So they cast, and then they were not able to haul it in because of the great number of fish.

2 Corinthians 9:8
And God is able to make all grace abound to you, so that always having all sufficiency in everything; you may have an abundance for every good deed;

Philippians 4:19
And my God will supply all your needs according to His riches in glory in Christ Jesus.

18. Prosper

As God's people we are called to prosper not to poverty. We are called to be the head and not the tail, to be above and not beneath. Prosperity is not wrong it is a blessing from God and if handled well will help in the extension of His kingdom as the Bible reminds us in 3 John 1:2 Beloved, I pray that you may prosper in all things and be in health, just as your soul prospers.

God's Word on the Matter:

Genesis 26:12
Then Isaac sowed in that land, and reaped in the same year a hundredfold; and the Lord blessed him

Genesis 39:3
Now his master saw that the Lord was with him and how the Lord caused all that he did to prosper in his hand.

Deuteronomy 8:18
…Remember the Lord your God, for it is He who gives you the ability to produce wealth.

Deuteronomy 15:10
You shall generously give to him, and your heart shall not be grieved when you give to him, because for this thing the Lord your God will bless you in all your work and in all your undertakings.

Deuteronomy 24:19
When you reap your harvest in your field and have forgotten a sheaf in the field, you shall not go back to get it; it shall be for the alien, for the orphan, and for the widow, in order that the Lord your God may bless you in all the work of your hands.

Deuteronomy 30:8-10
And you shall again obey the Lord, and observe all His commandments which I command you today. "Then the Lord your God will prosper you

abundantly in all the work of your hand, in the offspring of your body and in the offspring of your cattle and in the produce of your ground, for the Lord will again rejoice over you for good, just as He rejoiced over your fathers; if you obey the Lord your God to keep His commandments and His statutes which are written in this book of the law, if you turn to the Lord your God with all your heart and soul.

Joshua 1:8
This book of the law shall not depart from your mouth, but you shall meditate on it day and night, so that you may be careful to do according to all that is written in it; for then you will make your way prosperous, and then you will have success.

1 Chronicles 22:12
Only may the Lord give you wisdom and understanding, and give you charge concerning Israel, that you may keep the law of the Lord your God. Then you will prosper, if you take care

to fulfill the statutes and judgments with which the Lord charged Moses concerning Israel. Be strong and of good courage; do not fear nor be dismayed.

2 Chronicles 31:20
This is what Hezekiah did throughout Judah, doing what was good and right and faithful before the Lord his God. In everything that he undertook in the service of God's temple and in obedience to the law and the commands, he sought his God and worked wholeheartedly. And so he prospered.

Jeremiah 17:8
For he will be like a tree planted by the water, that extends its roots by a stream and will not fear when the heat comes; but its leaves will be green, and it will not be anxious in a year of drought nor cease to yield fruit.

Psalm 1: 1-3
Blessed is the man who does not walk in the

counsel of the wicked or stand in the way of sinners or sit in the seat of mockers. But his delight is in the law of the LORD, and on his law he meditates day and night. He is like a tree planted by streams of water, which yields its fruit in season and whose leaf does not wither. Whatever he does prospers.

Psalm 35:27
Let them shout for joy and rejoice, who favor my vindication; and let them say continually, "The Lord be magnified, who delights in the prosperity of His servant."

Proverbs 10:22
The blessing of the Lord makes one rich, and He adds no sorrow with it.

Malachi 3:10
"Bring all the tithes into the storehouse, that there may be food in My house, And try Me now in this", Says the Lord of hosts, "If I will not open for you the windows of heaven And pour

out for you such blessing that there will not be room enough to receive it."

Matthew 6:4
That your charitable deed may be in secret; and your Father who sees in secret will Himself reward you openly.

Matthew 19:29
And everyone who has left houses or brothers or sisters or father or mother or children or farms for My name's sake, will receive many times as much, and will inherit eternal life.

19. Receive

As much as we give to God we can and will also receive from Him, for He is a God who gives! As we become conduits of God's blessing we assist Him in giving to others. They will in turn receive in order to give and the cycle begins again!

God's Word on the Matter:

Ecclesiastes 5:19
Furthermore, as for every man to whom God has given riches and wealth, He has also empowered him to eat from them and to receive his reward and rejoice in his labor; this is the gift of God.

John 3:27
John answered and said, "A man can receive nothing unless it has been given him from heaven."

Acts 20:35
In everything I showed you that by working hard in this manner you must help the weak and remember the words of the Lord Jesus, that He Himself said, 'It is more blessed to give than to receive.'

1 Corinthians 9:10-11
Or is He speaking altogether for our sake? Yes, for our sake it was written, because the plowman ought to plow in hope, and the thresher to thresh in hope of sharing the crops. If we sowed spiritual things in you, is it too much if we reap material things from you?

1 Timothy 5:18
For the Scripture says, "Do not muzzle the ox while it is treading out the grain," and "The worker deserves his wages."

20. Save

Spending everything that we earn is not a good policy. We need to put something aside for a rainy day. It is wise to first give to God the 10% which belongs to Him. Next we need to save at least 20% of our income and then live on the remaining 70% not forgetting our freewill offerings. This 10-20-70 rule will help us provide a buffer for any future financial shock.

God's Word on the Matter:

Proverbs 21:5
The plans of the diligent lead surely to advantage, but everyone who is hasty comes surely to poverty.

Proverbs 21:20
There is precious treasure and oil in the dwelling of the wise, but a foolish man swallows it up.

Proverbs 27:12
A prudent man sees evil and hides himself, the naive proceed and pay the penalty

Proverbs 30:24-25
Four things are small on the earth, but they are exceedingly wise: The ants are not a strong people, but they prepare their food in the summer;

1 Corinthians 16:2
On the first day of every week each one of you is to put aside and save, as he may prosper, so that no collections be made when I come.

21. Strive for Success

Success should not be measured in monetary terms but in spiritual terms as we relate to God. Success in the spiritual realm is far more important to the Christian than anything else that this life has to offer. Be a success in everything that you do realising that ultimate success comes from knowing God. Why not prove Him at this time of recession, that in spite of how bad things look you can still find success in Him!

God's Word on the Matter:

Deuteronomy 30:9
The Lord your God will then make you successful in everything you do.

Joshua 1:8
This book of the law shall not depart from your mouth, but you shall meditate on it day and

night, so that you may be careful to do according to all that is written in it; for then you will make your way prosperous, and then you will have success.

Nehemiah 2:20
...The God of heaven will give us success; therefore we His servants will arise and build...

Psalm 1:1-3
Blessed is the man who does not walk in the counsel of the wicked or stand in the way of sinners or sit in the seat of mockers. But his delight is in the law of the Lord, and on his law he meditates day and night. He is like a tree planted by streams of water, which yields its fruit in season and whose leaf does not wither. Whatever he does prospers.

Psalm 37:4
Delight yourself in the Lord; And He will give you the desires of your heart.

Proverbs 22:29
Do you see a man skilled in his work? He will stand before kings; he will not stand before obscure men.

Proverbs 22:4
The reward of humility and the fear of the Lord are riches, honor and life.

Isaiah 1:19
If you consent and obey, you will eat the best of the land;

Matthew 6:24
No one can serve two masters; for either he will hate the one and love the other, or he will be devoted to one and despise the other you cannot serve God and wealth.

Matthew 23:12
Whoever exalts himself shall be humbled; and whoever humbles himself shall be exalted.

Luke 9:48
...and said to them, "Whoever receives this child in My name receives Me, and whoever receives Me receives Him who sent Me; for the one who is least among all of you, this is the one who is great."

Ephesians 3:20
Now to Him who is able to do far more abundantly beyond all that we ask or think, according to the power that works within us.

22. Being a Guarantor

Be careful of being a guarantor. Ask relevant questions and study the documentation. If in doubt, don't. Friends and family whom you trust now may abuse your trust later and cause you great distress and sink you into debt.

God's Word on the Matter:

Proverbs 6:1-2
My son, if you have become surety for your neighbor, have given a pledge for a stranger, if you have been snared with the words of your mouth, have been caught with the words of your mouth, then do this, my son, to free yourself, since you have fallen into your neighbor's hands: Go and humble yourself; press your plea with your neighbor!

Proverbs 11:15
He who is guarantor for a stranger will surely

suffer for it, but he who hates being a guarantor is secure.

Proverbs 17:18
A man lacking in sense pledges and becomes guarantor in the presence of his neighbor.

Proverbs 22:26-27
Do not be among those who give pledges, among those who become guarantors for debts. If you have nothing with which to pay, why should he take your bed from under you?

Proverbs 27:13
Take his garment when he becomes surety for a stranger; and for an adulterous woman hold him in pledge.

23. Satisfy Your Need Not Your Greed!

We live in a society that wants more and more. I once met a lady who told me that she had gone shopping and had bought a beautiful dress only to discover on arriving home, that she had purchased exactly the same dress sometime before and had totally forgotten about it!

We must learn to be satisfied with what we have and save up for what we really need. We must differentiate between our wants and our needs and know the difference. Are we needy or greedy?

The famous Aesop's Fable of "The Boy and the Nuts" tells of a little boy who once found a jar of nuts on the table. 'I would like some of these nuts," he thought. "I'm sure Mother would give them to me if she were here. I'll take a big handful," so he reached into the jar and grabbed as many as he could hold. But when he tried to pull his hand out, he found that the neck of the jar was too small. His hand was held fast, but he did not want to drop any of the nuts. He tried again and again, but he couldn't get the whole handful out. At last he began to cry.

Just then his mother came into the room. "What's the matter?" she asked. I can't take this handful of nuts out of the jar," sobbed the boy. "Well, don't be greedy," his mother replied. "Just take two or three, and you'll have no trouble getting your hand out." "How easy that was," said the boy as he left the table. "I should have thought of that myself."

We may want a lot but we can only handle so much at a time.

God's Word on the Matter:

Philippians 4:19
And my God will supply all your needs according to His riches in glory in Christ Jesus

24. Returning the Tithe

The Biblical principle of tithing is one of the surest things that we can use to beat back the tide of recession, for we are promised a blessing for our faithfulness.

The story is told of a lady who used to wash clothes for a living. One day as she was out looking for work she took her son along. As they went from house to house in search of work, but finding none, her son started to get hungry and asked for something to eat. His mother said she had no money to by any food. The boy reminded her that he had seen some money on the dresser. She then stated to him that that was the Lord's money. As they got home, still not finding any work and destine to go to bed hungry, the little boy asked again about the money on the dresser, the mother told him again it was the Lord's money and proceeded to ask him to take off her shoes. As he took off her shoes, what should he see stuck to the bottom of her shoe but a fifty pound note - enough money to buy food for the week! God will bless our faithfulness!

God's Word on the Matter:

Genesis 14:20
And blessed be God Most High, Who has delivered your enemies into your hand. He gave him a tenth of all.

Genesis 28:20-22
Then Jacob made a vow, saying, "If God will be with me and will keep me on this journey that I take, and will give me food to eat and garments to wear, and I return to my father's house in safety, then the Lord will be my God. "This stone, which I have set up as a pillar, will be God's house, and of all that You give me I will surely give a tenth to You."

Exodus 23:19
You shall bring the choice first fruits of your soil

into the house of the Lord your God You are not to boil a young goat in the milk of its mother.

Exodus 34:26
You shall bring the very first of the first fruits of your soil into the house of the Lord your God. You shall not boil a young goat in its mother's milk.

Leviticus 27:30
Thus all the tithe of the land, of the seed of the land or of the fruit of the tree, is the Lord's; it is holy to the Lord.

Numbers 18:26
Moreover, you shall speak to the Levites and say to them, 'When you take from the sons of Israel the tithe which I have given you from them for your inheritance, then you shall present an offering from it to the Lord.

Deuteronomy 14:22-23
You shall surely tithe all the produce from what

you sow, which comes out of the field every year. You shall eat in the presence of the Lord your God, at the place where He chooses to establish His name, the tithe of your grain, your new wine, your oil, and the firstborn of your herd and your flock, so that you may learn to fear the Lord your God always.

Deuteronomy 14:28
At the end of every third year you shall bring out all the tithe of your produce in that year, and shall deposit it in your town.

Deuteronomy 26:12
When you have finished paying all the tithe of your increase in the third year, the year of tithing, then you shall give it to the Levite, to the stranger, to the orphan and to the widow, that they may eat in your towns and be satisfied.

2 Chronicles 31:5
As soon as the order spread, the sons of Israel provided in abundance the first fruits of grain,

new wine, oil, honey and of all the produce of the field; and they brought in abundantly the tithe of all.

Nehemiah 10:38
The priest, the son of Aaron, shall be with the Levites when the Levites receive tithes, and the Levites shall bring up the tenth of the tithes to the house of our God, to the chambers of the storehouse.

Proverbs 3:9-10
Honor the Lord from your wealth and from the first of all your produce; so your barns will be filled with plenty and your vats will overflow with new wine.

Ezekiel 44:30
The first of all the first fruits of every kind and every contribution of every kind, from all your contributions, shall be for the priests; you shall also give to the priest the first of your dough to cause a blessing to rest on your house.

Amos 4:4
Enter Bethel and transgress; In Gilgal multiply transgression! Bring your sacrifices every morning, your tithes every three days.

Malachi 3:8-10
Will a man rob God? Yet you are robbing Me! But you say, 'How have we robbed You?' In tithes and offerings. "You are cursed with a curse, for you are robbing Me, the whole nation of you! Bring the whole tithe into the storehouse, so that there may be food in My house, and test Me now in this," says the LORD of hosts, "if I will not open for you the windows of heaven and pour out for you a blessing until it overflows?"

Matthew 23:23
Woe to you, scribes and Pharisees, hypocrites! For you tithe mint and dill and cummin, and have neglected the weightier provisions of the law: justice and mercy and faithfulness; but these are the things you should have done without neglecting the others.

1 Corinthians 16:1-2
Now concerning the collection for the saints, as I directed the churches of Galatia, so do you also. On the first day of every week each one of you is to put aside and save, as he may prosper, so that no collections be made when I come.

Hebrews 7:1-4
For this Melchizedek, king of Salem, priest of the Most High God, who met Abraham as he was returning from the slaughter of the kings and blessed him, to whom also Abraham apportioned a tenth part of all the spoils, was first of all, by the translation of his name, king of righteousness, and then also king of Salem, which is king of peace. Without father, without mother, without genealogy, having neither beginning of days nor end of life, but made like the Son of God, he remains a priest perpetually. Now observe how great this man was to whom Abraham, the patriarch, gave a tenth of the choicest spoils.

25. Let's Get to Work

My mother would often tell me as I did the chores around the house that hard work never killed anybody! We must work hard for the best things in life as nothing in life is for free!

God's Word on the Matter:

Genesis 2:15
Then the Lord God took the man and put him into the Garden of Eden to cultivate it and keep it.

Exodus 23:12
Six days you are to do your work, but on the seventh day you shall cease from labor so that your ox and your donkey may rest, and the son of your female slave, as well as your stranger, may refresh themselves.

2 Chronicles 31:21
Every work which he began in the service of

the house of God in law and in commandment, seeking his God, he did with all his heart and prospered.

Nehemiah 4:6
So we built the wall and the whole wall was joined together to half its height, for the people had a mind to work.

Psalm 127:2
It is vain for you to rise up early, to retire late, to eat the bread of painful labors; for He gives to His beloved even in his sleep.

Proverbs 10:4
Poor is he who works with a negligent hand, but the hand of the diligent makes rich.

Proverbs 12:14
A man will be satisfied with good by the fruit of his words, and the deeds of a man's hands will return to him.

Proverbs 12:24
The hand of the diligent will rule, but the slack

hand will be put to forced labor.

Proverbs 13:4
The soul of the sluggard craves and gets nothing, but the soul of the diligent is made fat.

Proverbs 13:11
Wealth obtained by fraud dwindles, but the one who gathers by labor increases it.

Proverbs 14:23
In all labor there is profit, but mere talk leads only to poverty.

Proverbs 18:9
He also who is slack in his work is brother to him who destroys.

Proverbs 20:4
The sluggard does not plow after the autumn, so he begs during the harvest and has nothing.

Proverbs 21:5
The plans of the diligent lead surely to

advantage, but everyone who is hasty comes surely to poverty.

Proverbs 21:25
The desire of the sluggard puts him to death, for his hands refuse to work;

Proverbs 22:29
Do you see a man skilled in his work? He will stand before kings; he will not stand before obscure men.

Proverbs 24:27
Prepare your work outside and make it ready for yourself in the field; Afterwards, then, build your house.

Proverbs 24:30-34
I passed by the field of the sluggard and by the vineyard of the man lacking sense, and behold, it was completely overgrown with thistles; its surface was covered with nettles, and its stone wall was broken down. When I saw, I reflected

upon it; I looked, and received instruction. "A little sleep, a little slumber, a little folding of the hands to rest," Then your poverty will come as a robber and your want like an armed man.

Proverbs 28:19
He who tills his land will have plenty of food, but he who follows empty pursuits will have poverty in plenty.

Ecclesiastes 5:12
The sleep of the working man is pleasant, whether he eats little or much; but the full stomach of the rich man does not allow him to sleep.

Ecclesiastes 9:10
Whatever your hand finds to do, do it with all your might; for there is no activity or planning or knowledge or wisdom in Sheol where you are going.

Ephesians 6:5-8
Slaves, be obedient to those who are your masters according to the flesh, with fear and trembling, in the sincerity of your heart, as to Christ; not by way of eye service, as men-pleasers, but as slaves of Christ, doing the will of God from the heart. With good will render service, as to the Lord, and not to men, knowing that whatever good thing each one does, this he will receive back from the Lord, whether slave or free.

Colossians 3:23
Whatever you do, do your work heartily, as for the Lord rather than for men,

1 Thessalonians 2:9
For you recall, brethren, our labor and hardship, how working night and day so as not to be a burden to any of you, we proclaimed to you the gospel of God.

2 Thessalonians 3:10-11
For even when we were with you, we used to give

you this order: if anyone is not willing to work, then he is not to eat, either. For we hear that some among you are leading an undisciplined life, doing no work at all, but acting like busybodies.

1 Timothy 5:8
But if anyone does not provide for his own, and especially for those of his household, he has denied the faith and is worse than an unbeliever.

Hebrews 6:10
For God is not unjust so as to forget your work and the love which you have shown toward His name, in having ministered and in still ministering to the saints.

26. Grow your Own

During these tough economic times everyone has to be thinking about how to make ends meet, how to save money and how to secure the food we put on our tables. Before the Second World War started Britain imported about 55 million tons of food a year from other countries. Understandably, the German government did what they could to disrupt this trade. One of the main methods used by the Germans was to get their battleships and submarines to hunt down and sink British merchant vessels.

With imports of food declining, the British government decided to introduce a system of rationing. This involved every householder registering with their local shops. The shopkeeper was then provided with enough food for his or her registered customers.

The government also introduced a Dig for

Victory campaign that called for every man and woman in Britain to keep an allotment. Lawns and flower-beds were turned into vegetable gardens. Over ten million instructional leaflets were distributed to the British people. The propaganda campaign was successful and it was estimated that over 1,400,000 people had allotments.

It is my belief that as a people we need to be moving towards a self sufficient lifestyle relying less on supermarkets and more on what we can produce for ourselves. We need to Dig for Victory! One of the ways we can do this is to grow our own food. There are a number of our members who have allotments and gardens that they use to grow food.

Ellen White states in the *Adventist Home*, p.141, Again and again the Lord has instructed that our people are to take their families away from the cities, into the country, where they can raise their own provision; for in the future the problem of buying and selling will be a very serious one.

Some of us may not be able to leave the cities now but we need to raise our own provision now!

It is time to get out in the garden and/or the allotment and get our hands dirty and wean ourselves off of the system before it is too late.

God's Word on the Matter:

Ezekiel 34:29
I will establish for them a renowned planting place, and they will not again be victims of famine in the land, and they will not endure the insults of the nations anymore.

Genesis 2:8
The LORD God planted a garden toward the east, in Eden; and there He placed the man whom He had formed.

Genesis 9:20
Then Noah began farming and planted a vineyard.

Genesis 21:33
Abraham planted a tamarisk tree at Beersheba, and there he called on the name of the LORD, the Everlasting God.

27. Give Thanks

It is always a good thing to give thanks particularly in these times. Giving thanks to God will actually keep you safe and sane when others are losing their minds!

God's Word on the Matter:

Philippians 4:6-7
Be anxious for nothing, but in everything by prayer and supplication with thanksgiving let your requests be made known to God. And the peace of God, which surpasses all comprehension, will guard your hearts and your minds in Christ Jesus.

Conclusion

We live unprecedented times, but we serve an all sufficient God who will never leave us or forsake us whilst as Luke 21:26 reminds us, men (will be) fainting from fear and the expectation of the things which are coming upon the world; for the powers of the heavens will be shaken.

We don't need to worry as the psalmist assures us in Psalm 46:1 God is our refuge and strength, a very present help in trouble. Therefore we will not fear, though the earth should change.

The world as we know it has changed and soon and very soon we will see Jesus. Let us hold on to the Word as is recorded in Psalm 119:105 as a lamp to my feet and a light to my path.

Let us continue to look up even though things are looking down and survive and thrive as a credit crunch christian.

NOTES

NOTES

NOTES

NOTES

NOTES

NOTES

NOTES

NOTES